Let's Get BLITZEN

60+ HOLIDAY COCKTAILS
TO MAKE YOUR SPIRITS BRIGHT

SOTHER TEAGUE

AUTHOR OF *I'M JUST HERE FOR THE DRINKS*

Deck the Halls
AND NOT YOUR IN-LAWS

The holiday season is, according to at least one Andy Williams song, the most wonderful time of the year. It can also be a complete Claus-terf**k. But don't let the worst of December turn you into a grinch. Break out your mixing glass and hold on to your winter cap because you're about to receive a sleigh's worth of liquid cheer to help you power through the New Year. This book has boozy recipes and shenanigans to keep you buzzing from the first dreidel spin to the ball drop. Just don't overdo it—no one wants to find you passed out under the tree Christmas morning.

—o •ᴑᎮᎾᴑ• o—

Contents

THESE LIBATIONS ARE AS
LINKED TO THE SEASON
AS HOLLY, IVY AND CRYING
ON SANTA'S LAP.

MULLED CIDER

This is a nonalcoholic

drink. But don't panic—you can add 2 ounces of rum, brandy or whiskey to your favorite mug then top it with this delightful tipple.

* Pour the apple cider into a 3-quart saucepan over medium heat. Cover.
* Peel your orange, then slice it into quarters. Stick the cloves into your orange slices in a way that seems festive, or just do it haphazard, it's your life.
* Place the orange, the peels and the rest of your cloves, as well as the remaining ingredients, into the saucepan with the cider. Cover and heat until the whole thing comes to a simmer. Reduce heat and let simmer for 20 to 30 minutes, or until you're thirsty for cider, whichever comes first.
* Use a mesh strainer to separate the cider from everything else and serve hot.

0.5 gallon fresh, unfiltered apple cider (nonalcoholic)

I orange

16 whole cloves

5 (3") sticks cinnamon

10 whole allspice berries

¼ tsp freshly ground nutmeg

5 cardamom pods

3 Tbsp demerara sugar

Garnish with a cinnamon stick.
And don't forget to add your favorite spirit.

MULLED WINE

Wine becomes something of a mixer in this wintry classic, a boozy favorite that'll have your whole house smelling of seasonal spices.

* Combine all ingredients in a large saucepan over medium heat.
* Bring to a simmer, then reduce heat to low. Let simmer for 20 to 30 minutes.
* Use a mesh strainer to separate wine from other ingredients, and serve in mugs.

Garnish with a slice of orange, a cinnamon stick or both.

Pro Tip If you make this mulled wine ahead of time it benefits from resting in your fridge overnight. Like opening presents on Christmas morning, there's pleasure to be had from the pain of waiting. Just reheat it before straining and serving. If you don't like to wait, well, don't. That goes for your presents too.

I cup sugar

2 oranges, sliced

¼ tsp freshly ground nutmeg

3 (3") sticks cinnamon

10 whole allspice berries

2–3 star anise pods

½ tsp whole peppercorns

5 whole cloves

I bottle (750 mL) red wine (go with a medium-bodied red blend, a merlot or a tempranillo)

I cup brandy

EGGNOG

You could buy those

premixed cartons of the stuff at your local grocery store, but making it yourself will give you something to brag about to everyone at your holiday party.

* Build in a mixer with ice.
* Whip-shake and strain.
* Serve in a wine glass.

Garnish with freshly grated nutmeg.

0.25 oz heavy cream

0.5 oz
demerara syrup

0.75 oz whole milk

I egg

0.5 oz Laird's
Apple Brandy

0.5 oz Jamaican rum

I oz Wild Turkey IOI
bourbon

Aged Eggnog

Whip up this nog once the holiday season rolls around, or—if you're feeling adventurous—make some in June and give aging it a try. If you are going to experiment with this approach, sanitizing the container you're going to use is the most important step. Use an airtight, sanitized container and fill it with as much nog as you can. I recommend a large glass bottle with an airtight lid. Once you've got the nog sealed tight, stick it in the fridge and basically forget all about it. (Like the rest of the condiments collecting goo in your fridge.)

From there, it's a waiting game. If you like, every week or so, give it a little shake. You don't want anything settling on the bottom, or anything with different densities resting on top of each other. You can store it in the refrigerator, but if you're feeling particularly adventurous, you can also age this eggnog in a dark, cool cabinet. The alcohol prevents any bacteria from taking hold. Aged eggnog makes a great gift, either for friends, family or yourself.

"MERRY CHRISTMAS, ya filthy ANIMAL."

—Home Alone 2

HOT TODDY

A holiday classic that

works well all winter, a toddy is the perfect cure for a lingering cold or that rambling uncle who can't wait to tell you a story you've heard him share 34 times.

2 tsp demerara sugar or brown sugar

0.25 oz fresh lemon juice

2 oz blended scotch

I lemon wheel

4 whole cloves

Boiling water

* Boil some water. While it's boiling, cut a lemon wheel and dot it with four whole cloves.
* Add sugar to about half a mug-full of boiling water and stir to dissolve.
* Add the prepared lemon wheel and stir some more.
* Add the lemon juice and whiskey, then stir again.
* Stir one last time just to make sure you're following directions, then serve.

Pro Tip For better results, prime the mug you're planning to serve this drink in by heating it up with some boiling water. After 2 to 3 minutes, discard that water and then build your drink in a piping-hot mug.

HOT BUTTERED RUM

With a history that dates back to the Colonial period, this comforting classic has been a part of Christmas longer than those hideous sweaters. This recipe makes four servings (or one serving if you're celebrating alone).

* Combine all ingredients in a medium saucepan over high heat and bring to a boil, then reduce heat and let simmer for 10 minutes, stirring occasionally.
* Serve warm.

Garnish with a cinnamon stick.

2 cups water

½ stick unsalted butter

¼ cup packed dark brown sugar

I tsp cinnamon

½ tsp freshly grated nutmeg

½ tsp ground cloves

¼ tsp salt

I cup dark rum

Pro Tip You can top with whipped cream or a drop of half-and-half for a richer treat..

WHITE RUSSIAN

The Big Lebowski is

basically a Christmas movie:
A jolly man with a beard and an
aging veteran help a youngster
learn the consequences of taking
advantage of a stranger, while
simultaneously doing a good
deed for a man in a wheelchair.
Admittedly, the illusion works
better if you've been pounding
White Russians. This drink features
prominently throughout the film,
and is also the perfect treat to
leave alongside Santa's cookies.

I oz Kahlúa or your
favorite coffee liqueur

2 oz vodka

Heavy cream

* Combine the vodka and liqueur in a
rocks glass over ice. Top with a splash
of heavy cream and stir to combine.

*Garnish with freshly grated
nutmeg for extra holiday flavor.*

Unpopular Lessons from Popular Christmas Movies

Films taking place around Jesus's birthday
sure do have some unholy takeaways.

It's a Wonderful Life

All it takes to ruin Christmas is the disappearance
of an average white guy.

The Santa Clause

The only way to earn your son's love is to become
a completely different person.

How the Grinch Stole Christmas

In order to save your loved ones from the highly
commercialized marketing season, just steal all their
food and presents and decorations and furniture.
That'll show 'em.

A Christmas Story

The best and most memorable way to solve your
problems is by weaving a tapestry of profanity.

The Family Stone

All it takes to bring a disparate family together
is the holiday season and hatred of Sarah Jessica Parker.

Rudolph the Red-Nosed Reindeer

Accept everyone's differences (but only when you
need to take advantage of them).

Love Actually

On Christmas Eve, there's nothing more romantic
than trying to seduce your best friend's wife.

BOURBON HOT CHOCOLATE

Some nights, nothing beats a warm mug of delicious cocoa—except the very same with a shot of bourbon in it. This recipe includes a cocoa mix of my own creation and features just a touch of cayenne pepper for an extra kick.

2 Tbsp Sother's Cocoa Mix (see below)

3 oz hot milk

2 oz Wild Turkey 101 bourbon

* Combine all ingredients in a mug and enjoy!
* Top with marshmallows.

SOTHER'S COCOA MIX

* Combine all ingredients.
* Add 5 ounces of warm milk (or 3 ounces milk and 2 ounces bourbon) to 2 tablespoons of mix for hot cocoa.

2 cups powdered sugar

I cup cocoa (Dutch-process preferred)

2½ cups powdered milk

I tsp salt

2 tsp cornstarch

¼ tsp cayenne pepper, or more to taste

"AREN'T WE FORGETTING THE TRUE meaning OF THIS DAY? The birth of SANTA?"

— The Simpsons

THE SEELBACH

Named after a fancy
hotel in Louisville, Kentucky,
where this cocktail was created,
its origin story suggests it was
discovered by accident in 1912
when the barman accidentally
spilled a honeymooning groom's
Manhattan into the bride's glass
of Champagne. It's a lovely story,
but also totally made up—
a marketing trick to push more
merchandise. It's also red. What's
more Christmas-y than that?

7 dashes
Angostura bitters

7 dashes
Peychaud's Bitters

0.5 oz triple sec

I oz bourbon,
preferably Old Forester

5 oz domestic
Brut sparkling
wine, preferably
Korbel Brut, chilled

＊In a mixing glass filled three-
quarters with ice, combine the first
four ingredients. Stir until chilled,
about 30 seconds.

＊Strain the mixture into a Champagne
flute. Top with the sparkling wine.

Garnish with an orange twist.

Pro Tip This drink is best when all
its ingredients are cold, so don't skip
step one, thirst be damned.

"**SAY YOU HATE** *Washington's birthday* or **THANKSGIVING AND NOBODY CARES,** *but say you hate* **CHRISTMAS AND EVERYBODY MAKES** *you feel like* **YOU'RE A LEPER.**"

—Gremlins

IRISH COFFEE

There's nothing worse than a bad cup of coffee, and if there's one thing the holidays are lousy with, it's burnt pots of Folgers masquerading as quality Kona. No matter how tar-like your in-laws' morning pick-me-ups might be, you can elevate any cup of coffee by adding a bit of Irish whiskey.

Freshly brewed coffee

1 Tbsp demerara sugar

2 oz Irish whiskey

Whipped cream

* Fill a mug about three-quarters of the way full with hot coffee. Add the sugar and stir until dissolved. Add whiskey and stir.
* Top with whipped cream and serve.

Pro Tip You can use Cool Whip or that spray whipped cream that's likely in your fridge somewhere during the holiday season, but you can also make your own whipped cream by adding 0.5 ounces simple syrup to 4 ounces heavy cream (plus a little vanilla extract for flavor), then shaking the hell out of it.

Your Family's Holiday Drinking Game

I don't know the people you spend this season with, but you do. Use the template below to create your own drinking game based on the people you love (or at least are planning to spend time with).

Every time _____ cries, take a shot.

Whenever _____ plays on the radio, take a sip.

If you hear the phrase "_____," finish your drink.

If _____ asks you how to do something on their new electronic device, take a shot.

Every time _____ makes a sweeping generalization, finish your drink.

Whenever _____'s new toy makes a sound, take a sip.

Every time _____ shows you pictures of their pet(s), take a sip.

If _____ tells a story about _____, finish your drink.

If _____ gives you _____ for the _____ year in a row, take a sip.

Every time _____ sneaks food to _____ (insert name of child or family pet), take a sip.

Every time _____ asks when _____ will get married or have a baby, finish THEIR drink.

If _____ and _____ get into an argument, take a shot—or three.

When you see a commercial for _____, take a sip.

Whenever _____ side-eyes the presents, take a shot.

When _____ offers a backhanded compliment, take a sip.

If _____ mentions Frank Capra was a communist, finish your drink.

BRANDY ALEXANDER

A perfect blend of chocolate, cream and booze, this classic cocktail is a bit more elegant than a White Russian, but that doesn't mean you can't enjoy it while wearing a bathrobe, the unofficial Christmas morning uniform of dads everywhere.

0.75 oz heavy cream

I oz crème de cacao

1.25 oz brandy

＊ Shake vigorously with ice to chill, dilute and emulsify. Strain into a chilled cocktail glass.

Garnish with grated nutmeg.

"Can I refill your EGGNOG for YOU? Get you something TO EAT? Drive you out to THE MIDDLE OF NOWHERE and leave you for ✳ DEAD?"

—National Lampoon's Christmas Vacation

POINSETTIA

Named after a flower popular for Christmas decorations (which was named after a Carolinian politician and our first ambassador to Mexico, John R. Poinsett), the Poinsettia is about as simple to create as it is easy to consume. Enjoy it while doing your best not to discuss politics.

3 oz cranberry juice

0.5 oz triple sec

Sparkling wine (Champagne or a fruity cava)

* Mix the triple sec and cranberry juice in a Champagne glass, then top slowly with sparkling wine.

Garnish with dried cranberries and a rosemary sprig.

PRO TIP If you're throwing a New Year's Eve party (or New Year's Day brunch), this is a fantastic drink to make ahead of time. Just mix a whole pitcher full of the cranberry juice and triple sec (at a 6-to-1 ratio) and leave it in the fridge overnight. When you're ready to serve, pour the mix into your glasses, top with bubbles, garnish and serve.

"Ahh, smell those Christmas trees. YOU CAN KEEP your 'Channel No. 5,' JUST GIVE ME A WHIFF OF THE OLD LONESOME PINE. That symbol of brotherly love, THAT CENTERPIECE that all mankind gathers around to share the cranberry sauce SHAPED LIKE A CAN."

—Ernest Saves Christmas

BAKED APPLE TODDY

If Starbucks can push pumpkin spice lattes on us during August, you should be allowed to drink this autumnal stunner well into winter. And you will. Because it's damn good.

* Add all ingredients to a mug.

Garnish with fresh nutmeg and an apple chip.

2 dashes Greenbar Organic Apple Bitters

0.25 oz lemon juice

0.5 oz cinnamon syrup

I oz hot apple cider

1.5 oz Laird's Apple Brandy

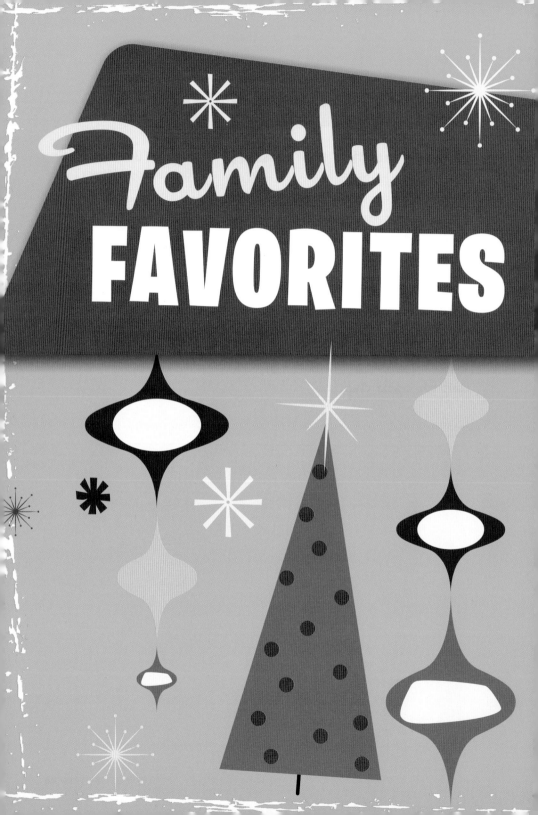

Family FAVORITES

YOU DON'T NEED TO KNOW
HOW TO MAKE EVERY COCKTAIL
EVER INVENTED—JUST THE ONES
YOUR GUESTS ARE MOST LIKELY
TO ASK FOR BY NAME.

OLD-FASHIONED

A phrase almost always followed by a deeply held view about people of another race, class or circumstance, "Call me old-fashioned, but..." can easily be interpreted as a request for this classic. Before they can offer you a wide-ranging but narrow-minded opinion, just hand them this drink instead.

Dash Angostura bitters

Dash orange bitters

2 oz rye

Spoonful demerara or cane syrup

* Combine all ingredients in an Old-Fashioned glass.
* Add one large-format ice cube.
* Stir to combine.

Garnish with a lemon twist.

Pro Tip One of the earliest cocktails in the canon, the Old-Fashioned is also one of the easiest to riff on. Try different blends of whiskey or other spirits entirely, as well as garnishes, and develop a cocktail of your own.

NEGRONI

When your salty aunt

won't stop judging you, pour two Negronis—one for you and one for her. Things will either quiet down or get a little spicy.

* Combine all ingredients in a rocks glass.
* Add one large-format ice cube.
* Stir to combine.

Garnish with an orange twist.

1 ½ dashes
Angostura bitters

0.75 oz Campari

0.75 oz sweet vermouth

1.5 oz London dry gin

GEORGE: OH, HELLO, NICK. HEY, WHERE'S MARTINI?

NICK: YOU WANT A MARTINI?

GEORGE: NO, NO, MARTINI. YOUR BOSS. WHERE IS HE?

NICK: LOOK, I'M THE BOSS. YOU WANT A DRINK OR DON'T YOU?

GEORGE: OK... ALL RIGHT. DOUBLE BOURBON, QUICK, HUH?

—It's a Wonderful Life

MARTINI

When you've seen one
too many Christmas movies, purge yourself of the holiday schmaltz with this clean, crisp cocktail. Bonus: It isn't red or green!

2 dashes orange bitters

1.5 oz Dolin dry vermouth

1.5 oz London dry gin

* Stir all ingredients with plenty of ice in a large mixing glass to both chill and dilute.
* Strain into a chilled cocktail glass.

Garnish with a lemon twist.

Pro Tip The martini is a gin cocktail, and always has been. If a member of your family asks for a "vodka martini" tell them there's no such thing (a mix of vodka and dry vermouth is called "the Kangaroo Cocktail") and lord your superiority over them for the rest of the holiday season. Or just keep it to yourself.

On Ice

With very few exceptions, ice is a major component of every cocktail you'll ever make or drink, which is why you should use the best ice you can.

Because modern freezers create ice so quickly, oxygen doesn't have time to escape—which explains those big white clouds present in nearly every cube. And if the air inside your freezer is trapped inside your ice, that means the smell inside your freezer is trapped inside it too. The smell of a year-old frozen turkey leg, the wet cardboard tang of a nearly finished Häagen-Dazs pint and the essence of that weird blue gel pack intertwine in the ice and infiltrate your cocktail as it begins to melt. And because the ice has air pockets inside it, it'll melt faster than ice created in the natural world. If you're particular about ice—and you should be, given everything you just learned—you may want to consider buying some or freezing it in a sealable container on its own, away from the other contaminants in your freezer. Which you should also clean.

DAIQUIRI

Always a crowd pleaser,
the Daiquiri will have your guests smiling long after someone's brought up politics. If someone complains you're serving these instead of Champagne for a toast, tell them the ball just dropped on their invitation.

0.75 oz lime juice

0.75 oz simple syrup

1.5 oz white rum

* Shake all ingredients together with ice.
* Double strain into a chilled coupe glass.

Garnish with a lime wedge.

Pro Tip The Daiquiri is a simple template that's easy to replicate but somewhat unforgiving if your ingredients aren't of a decent quality. In other words, use fresh juice and better-than-average rum—the type you might buy someone as a gift, before opening it and mixing a drink for yourself.

SAZERAC

A little sweet, somewhat bitter—sounds like holiday guests to us. This Crescent City classic will cater to the needs of either camp.

Absinthe or Herbsaint

2 dashes
Peychaud's Bitters

0.5 oz simple syrup

2 oz rye whiskey

* Give a chilled glass an absinthe or Herbsaint rinse and set aside.
* Stir the other ingredients in a mixing glass and strain into the chilled glass.

Garnish with a lemon twist.

Pro Tip "Rinsing" a glass means adding a little booze to it, swirling that booze around, then dumping it. This technique adds a hint of flavor, but not enough to overpower your drink.

WHISKEY SOUR

Lost that Christmas

spirit? Feel all warm and fuzzy again courtesy of this relaxing refresher. But pace yourself— drinking sours is no excuse to be a grump.

0.75 oz lemon juice

0.75 oz simple syrup

2 oz rye or bourbon

*Shake with ice and strain into a chilled cocktail glass.

Garnish with lemon and cherry.

"IN THE HEAT OF BATTLE * **my father wove a tapestry of obscenity THAT, AS FAR AS WE KNOW,** * is still hanging in space **OVER LAKE MICHIGAN. "**

*

—A Christmas Story

FRENCH 75

An old French tradition

on Christmas Eve involves downing three of these in a row while devouring Christmas cookies. Or is that just Aunt Peg's tradition? Either way, make it yours.

0.5 oz simple syrup

0.75 oz lemon juice

1.5 oz gin

Chilled Champagne

* Shake first three ingredients with ice.
* Strain into a chilled Champagne flute.
* Top it off with Champagne and serve.

No garnish.

Pro Tip You can add a little elegance to almost any cocktail by topping it with a little Champagne. Note: In this case "elegance" means "more booze."

"HALLELUJAH! HOLY SHIT! * Where's THE TYLENOL?*"

—National Lampoon's Christmas Vacation

GIMLET

Gimlet has the same

number of letters as Grinch. It's also green. Boom. Holidays. While I can't promise you won't steal all the presents after you've had a few of these, you'll definitely start talking to your dog.

0.75 oz simple syrup

0.75 oz lime juice

1.5 oz gin

* Shake with ice and strain into a chilled cocktail glass.

No garnish.

Family Holiday Dos and Don'ts

For starters, don't get together without access to this list (and these drinks).

DO Compliment your cousin's experimental casserole.
DON'T Actually eat any of it.

DO Swallow your pride and join in singing Christmas songs.
DON'T Join your mother-in-law in a duet of "Baby It's Cold Outside."

DO Bring dessert.
DON'T Be the fruitcake guy.

DO Excitedly anticipate your family opening the gifts you gave them.
DON'T Tell them they're all re-gifts.

DO Watch an underrated Christmas movie that's not about Christmas.

DON'T Let it be *Eyes Wide Shut*.

DO Get comfortable sleeping in your S.O.'s creepy, nostalgia-ridden childhood bedroom.
DON'T Ask their sibling to join you.

DO Open the oven before removing freshly baked cookies.
DON'T Stick your head inside to escape your family gathering Sylvia Plath–style.

DO Share your favorite memories featuring Christmas mornings past.
DON'T Share your favorite memories featuring Christmas morning hangovers.

COSMOPOLITAN

Holiday shopping is
rough. Couldn't snag the
perfect gift? Pour yourself
a Cosmo and forget who
you forgot on your list.

0.5 oz cranberry juice

0.5 oz lime juice

0.5 oz triple sec

1.5 oz vodka

✳ Shake well with ice and strain into a
chilled cocktail glass.

Garnish with lime.

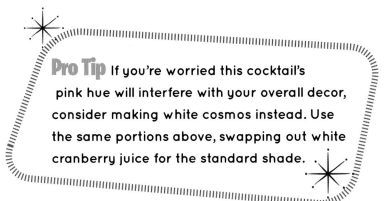

Pro Tip If you're worried this cocktail's
pink hue will interfere with your overall decor,
consider making white cosmos instead. Use
the same portions above, swapping out white
cranberry juice for the standard shade.

MANHATTAN

You'll have to travel to Brooklyn's Grand Army Plaza to see one of the world's largest menorahs, but you can make a delicious Manhattan at home.

* Stir in a mixing glass to chill and combine.
* Strain into a chilled cocktail glass.

Garnish with cherry or lemon twist.

2 dashes
Angostura bitters

I oz sweet vermouth

2 oz rye

MARTINEZ

The lush, rosy Martinez

will keep you merry and bright long after your family has overstayed their welcome. Add two dashes of gum syrup for an even sweeter treat.

❋ Shake thoroughly with ice and strain into a chilled cocktail glass.

Garnish with lemon.

I dash Boker's Bitters

0.25 oz
Maraschino liqueur

1.5 oz of sweet
vermouth

1.5 oz Old Tom gin

"WHO DO YOU have to screw AROUND HERE TO GET A cup of tea and a chocolate biscuit?,,

—Love Actually

SIDECAR

Winter days are short and dark. When you're neck-deep in snow, ignore the frostbite with this light, citrusy cocktail. But also get inside. You could die.

0.75 oz fresh lemon juice

0.75 oz triple sec

2 oz Cognac

* Shake with ice and strain into a chilled cocktail glass.

"WHO GAVE YOU * PERMISSION TO TELL CHARLIE there was no Santa Claus? **I THINK IF WE'RE GOING TO DESTROY** our son's delusions ***I SHOULD BE A PART OF IT.*"**

— The Santa Clause

CORPSE REVIVER NO. 2

A cocktail originally envisioned as a day-starter following a night of heavy drinking, you'll welcome this one on New Year's morning. Or New Year's Eve. Or any day, really.

* Shake with ice and strain in a chilled cocktail glass.

No garnish.

0.75 oz lemon juice

0.75 oz triple sec

0.75 oz Lillet Blanc

0.75 oz gin

I dash of absinthe or pastis

Shiny
NEW TOYS

MANY OF THESE DRINKS ARE JUST LIKE ITEMS ON YOUR GIFT LIST—MODERN VERSIONS OF STUFF THAT WORKS BUT COULD USE AN UPDATE.

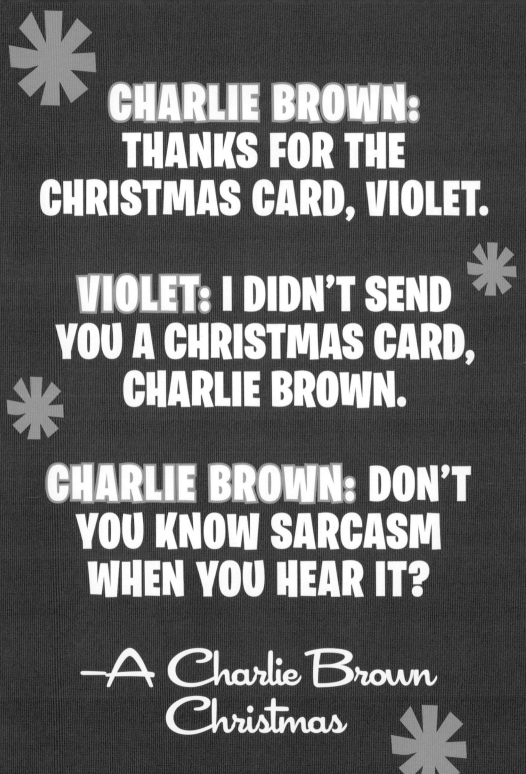

CHARLIE BROWN:
THANKS FOR THE
CHRISTMAS CARD, VIOLET.

VIOLET: I DIDN'T SEND
YOU A CHRISTMAS CARD,
CHARLIE BROWN.

CHARLIE BROWN: DON'T
YOU KNOW SARCASM
WHEN YOU HEAR IT?

—A Charlie Brown
Christmas

MOSCOW REINDEER

Rudolph's famously freakish nose is red and yours will be too after downing a few of these mixed-up Moscow Mules.

0.75 oz cranberry juice

2 oz vodka

Ginger beer

* Combine first two ingredients over ice in a copper mug.
* Top with ginger beer.

Garnish with fresh rosemary.

Pro Tip When adding the rosemary sprig as a garnish, give it a good slap between your hands to release a bit more of its telltale scent.

||||||||||||||||||||||||||||| ✳ |||||||||||||||||||||||||||||

CLARK: OUR HOLIDAYS WERE ALWAYS SUCH A MESS.

CLARK SR.: OH, YEAH.

CLARK: HOW'D YOU GET THROUGH IT?

CLARK SR.: I HAD A LOT OF HELP FROM JACK DANIELS.

||||||||||||||||||||||||||||| ✳ |||||||||||||||||||||||||||||

—National Lampoon's Christmas Vacation

SCROOGE-DRIVER

Drown your need to say
"bah humbug" with plenty of vodka and vitamin C. Juicing the oranges with the pith still on the flesh adds an Ebeneezer-worthy touch of bitterness and also a lovely bit of foam for texture.

I medium orange, peeled with pith intact

2 oz vodka

* Push orange through high-speed juicer.
* Pour OJ and chilled vodka into a highball glass.

Garnish with an orange slice.

Pro Tip If you don't have access to a Breville juicer because you are a normal person who doesn't have a restaurant in their home, 1) Ask for one for Christmas, or 2) Just peel the orange down to the pith and cut into small chunks, then toss them in your blender. Purée until smooth and strain through a fine mesh strainer before proceeding.

" Now I have a
MACHINE GUN.

HO
HO
HO.

"

-Die Hard

NAUGHTY MARTINI

Feeling salty about blowing your chances of making the Nice List this year? Look no further than this briny brew.

0.5 oz olive brine

1 oz Dolin dry vermouth

1.5 oz London dry gin

* Stir all ingredients with plenty of ice in a large mixing glass to both chill and dilute.
* Strain into a chilled cocktail glass.

Garnish with blue cheese-stuffed olives.

Pro Tip Most folks who order a Dirty Martini want it with extra olives, so it's a good idea to garnish with three by default.

5 Best Christmas Movies That Aren't About Christmas

When you've already screened every traditional Christmas movie and it isn't even Christmas Eve, check out these holiday-adjacent favorites.

Gremlins Who says a horror film can't be a Christmas flick? This classic explores the nightmare that unfolds when your Christmas present from dad torments your town.

Kiss Kiss Bang Bang This festive murder mystery stars Robert Downey Jr.—pulling a reverse Winona Ryder—as a thief who becomes an actor after getting caught trying to steal a gift for his kid.

Die Hard and **Die Hard 2: Die Harder** Nobody embraces the Christmas spirit quite like Bruce Willis's John McClane when he saves his wife from her terrible office party on Christmas Eve. Need more season's beatings? The sequel sees McClane stab a guy in the eye with an icicle and pursue perps in a snowmobile chase after getting stuck at the airport on Christmas. Yippee-ki-yay!

Lethal Weapon Christmas is in the periphery of this buddy cop classic: "Jingle Bell Rock" plays as someone falls to their death and there's a drug bust scene that takes place in a Christmas tree lot. Family fun!

LAZY DESSERT

Sure, you could go all-out and make a decadent holiday spread that would make Julia Child proud, or you could shake up some ice cream and gin, grab a straw and go to town. It's the holiday season. You can do both.

2 oz mint chip ice cream (softened)

1.5 oz London dry gin

0.5 oz Branca Menta (optional...if you're feeling lazy)

* Add to a shaker and whip to combine.
* Add a metal straw and drink directly from the shaker tin.

No garnish.

"I PASSED THROUGH the seven levels of the CANDY CANE FOREST, THROUGH THE sea of swirly twirly GUMDROPS and then I walked through THE LINCOLN TUNNEL."

—Elf

RED GIN

A gin Old-Fashioned

wrapped in a big red bow courtesy of the cinnamon and vanilla in Peychaud's, this drink is truly a gift that keeps on giving.

* Combine all ingredients into an Old-Fashioned glass.
* Add ice and stir a few times to combine.

Garnish with a lemon twist.

3 dashes Peychaud's bitters

0.25 oz homemade grenadine (see below)

1.5 oz London dry gin

Splash of seltzer

HOMEMADE GRENADINE

* Over medium heat, reduce the juice by half to 1 cup. Meanwhile, peel the oranges down to the white pith.
* Stir in the sugar to dissolve.
* Add orange peels and remove from heat.
* Cover and allow to cool.
* Stir in orange flower water to taste.
* Strain and refrigerate.
* Will last three weeks refrigerated. Shelf life can be extended by adding 1 oz of an overproof spirit such as vodka.

2 cups pomegranate juice

2 cups sugar

4 medium sized oranges

1–2 tsp orange flower water

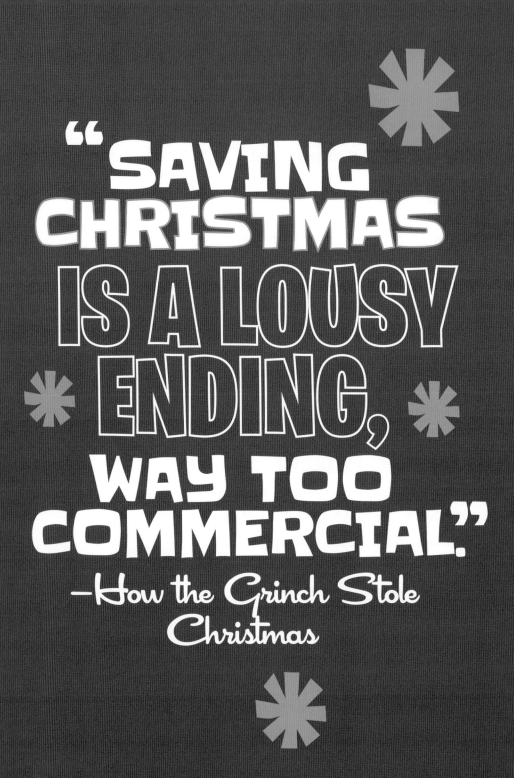

"SAVING CHRISTMAS IS A LOUSY ENDING, WAY TOO COMMERCIAL."

—How the Grinch Stole Christmas

BURNIN' LOVE

When the Christmas

season feels like hell (Santa and Satan are one letter off, after all), get lit with this drink that you can actually set on fire—courtesy of an irresistible herbal liqueur—while everything else goes up in metaphorical flames.

Fresh thyme sprig

0.5 oz Green Chartreuse

0.5 oz lime juice

0.5 oz maraschino liqueur

1 oz Plymouth gin

* Place thyme into a heavy rocks glass and pour in Chartreuse.
* Pour all remaining ingredients into a shaker tin with ice.
* Using a long match or torch, light the thyme on fire.
* Shake the tin as the thyme burns.
* Pour the shaker's contents, ice and all, over the burning thyme to extinguish the flames.

Garnish with fresh thyme sprig.

CAMPFIRE OLD-FASHIONED

You can almost smell the smoke in this spicy, peaty classic—or is that the Yule log? You might want to check on your tree just in case. Then finish this drink.

* Add ingredients to an Old-Fashioned glass.
* Add a large lump of ice and gently stir to combine.

Garnish with a flamed orange twist.

Dash Angostura bitters

Dash Bittermens Hellfire Habanero Shrub

1.5 tsp cane syrup

0.25 oz peated scotch

0.75 oz rye

0.75 oz bourbon

Pro Tip You can flame an orange twist by holding a lit match over the top of your cocktail and expressing the oil from the twist so it passes through the flame and ignites on its way into the glass. Note: Don't do this anywhere near your Christmas tree.

IMPROVED HOLLAND'S OLD-FASHIONED

With herbal absinthe, a hint of cherries and Old Duff Genever, this updated version of an absolute throwback tastes like the holidays smell.

* Add all ingredients to a mixing glass with plenty of ice.
* Stir to chill and dilute, then strain into a chilled cocktail glass.

Garnish with a lemon twist.

2 dashes Angostura bitters

1.5 tsp demerara syrup

4 dashes absinthe

4 dashes maraschino

2 oz Old Duff Genever

"**PUT THAT cookie DOWN, NOW!**"

—Jingle All the Way

PUMPERNICKEL

You may be having

challah as part of your Hanukkah gatherings, but you can still savor the flavors of your favorite pumpernickel rye with this deep-hued, spicy take on the Manhattan that tastes just like its namesake from your favorite deli.

7 dashes (yup, 7) Angostura bitters

0.5 oz Punt e Mes

0.75 oz Amaro Abano

1.5 oz 100° rye whiskey

* Stir ingredients with plenty of ice to chill and dilute.
* Strain into a chilled glass.

Lemon twist, discarded.

5 Christmas Songs That Should Be Destroyed

These ubiquitous holiday jingles should be banned to the Island of Misfit Tunes.

"Wonderful Christmastime"
by Paul McCartney

Paul insists things are great but the sleazy synthezisers say otherwise. Stop telling us things are wonderful, you gaslighting Beatle bastard.

"All I Want For Christmas Is You"
by Mariah Carey & Justin Bieber

Let's agree whoever thought Justin Bieber could improve on holiday pop perfection should have their name engraved on the Naughty List.

"The Christmas Shoes"
by NewSong

Encouraging people to help others during the holidays is great, but this dying mother anthem feels like being told to do good at gunpoint.

"Grandma Got Run Over By a Reindeer"
by Elmo & Patsy

The crown jewel in the "Family Killed on Christmas Eve" holiday music subgenre, this tune raises important questions about plausible deniability.

"Happy Xmas (War Is Over)"
by John Lennon & Yoko Ono

War and this song's unbearable ubiquity persist.

SOUTHERN BAPTIST

Does the thought of

going to church have you feeling shook? Take the edge off by shaking this rye whiskey and ginger syrup highball, then pour it straight into your mouth.

0.75 oz fresh lime juice

0.75 oz ginger syrup (see below)

2 oz rye

* Combine all ingredients in a shaker. Then add ice.
* Shake vigorously and double strain into a cocktail glass.

Garnish with candied ginger.

||||||||||||||||||||||||||||||||||||||||||||||||||||||||||||||||||||||||||||||||||||

GINGER SYRUP

* Combine sugar and ginger juice over heat.
* Bring to a simmer and stir to dissolve sugar.
* Allow to cool to room temperature.
* Store in the fridge.

I cup sugar

I cup ginger juice (you can source from your local juice shop)

HUMBUG

Make up for all the
years you were an absolute Scrooge by serving this cocktail that's as rich and complex as you are.

* Muddle the green cardamom pod with the syrup.
* Add remaining ingredients and ice, shake and double strain into a cocktail glass.

Garnish with drops of Angostura Bitters.

I green cardamom pod

0.25 oz heavy cinnamon clove syrup (see below)

0.5 oz pineapple juice

0.5 oz lemon juice

I oz Wild Turkey Rye

Pro Tip The recipe below can serve as a template for any "infused" syrup. Want to make an allspice syrup? Throw some allspice berries into the simmering water and make magic. Cover the syrup as it cools to enhance the infusion.

HEAVY CINNAMON CLOVE SYRUP

* Combine sugar and water over heat.
* Bring to a simmer and add cinnamon sticks and cloves.
* Stir to dissolve sugar.
* Cover and allow to cool to room temperature.
* Strain and store in the fridge.

I cup sugar

I cup water

5 sticks cinnamon

I tsp whole cloves

RYE CAPPUCCINO

Whether you plan on
staying up to see Santa or just need a little jolt to make it through Christmas Eve (or Christmas morning, or New Year's), this creamy, caffeinated cocktail will have you flying faster than Blitzen himself.

2 dashes chocolate bitters

I oz cold espresso

0.5 oz brown sugar syrup (see below)

2 oz rye

0.75 oz heavy cream

* Shake first three ingredients and strain into a chilled cordial glass.
* Shake cream and bitters in a tin without ice to whip.
* Float cream on top.

Garnish with dark chocolate espresso beans.

BROWN SUGAR SYRUP
* Combine sugar and water over heat.
* Bring to a simmer and stir to dissolve sugar.
* Allow to cool to room temperature.
* Store in the fridge.

2 cups dark brown sugar

I cup water

CAFÉ BRÛLÉE

Cold brew coffee is the key ingredient in this drink that'll have you even more wired than your over-the-top Christmas light display.

* In a double old-fashioned glass add first four ingredients.
* Place a large lump of ice in the glass and gently stir to combine.
* Sprinkle the salt on top.

No garnish.

0.5 oz cold brew coffee

1.5 tsp burnt sugar syrup (see below)

1.5 oz Cognac

2 dashes vanilla bitters

Pinch smoked salt or Maldon salt

BURNT SUGAR SYRUP

* Place sugar in a medium saucepan over high heat.
* Stirring constantly, cook until the sugar melts, about 5 minutes.
* Cook until dark brown and foamy with wisps of smoke. Remove from heat.
* Stirring constantly, pour in the hot water. It will splatter a lot, so be careful.
* Once fully incorporated, return to medium-high heat and cook until the syrup thickens slightly. Cool completely before use.

1 cup granulated white sugar

0.75 cup very hot water

"You call this a **HAPPY FAMILY?** Why do we have to have all **THESE KIDS?**"

—*It's a Wonderful Life*

TEATRO

When your house is packed to the rafters with bickering relatives, ask something banal like, "So what should we do about the border?" Then sit back and watch the holiday drama unfold with a Teatro (Spanish for theater, which is basically what your house is now, compadre).

2 dashes orange bitters

I oz sweet vermouth

I oz Green Chartreuse

I oz Olmeca Altos Tequila Blanco

* Stir all ingredients with ice.
* Strain into a cocktail glass over ice.

Garnish with cherries.

"THERE'S CHILDREN THROWING SNOWBALLS, INSTEAD OF THROWING HEADS. THEY'RE BUSY BUILDING TOYS, AND ABSOLUTELY NO ONE'S DEAD!"

—The Nightmare Before Christmas

ROSARITA

This tequila-based cocktail comes decked out in red and green, making for one snazzy Christmas libation with an added sour kick. A refreshing palate cleanser after one too many Christmas cookies.

1.5 oz raspberry shrub (see below)

2 dashes absinthe

2 oz blanco tequila

3 basil leaves

* Shake all ingredients together with ice.
* Strain into an old-fashioned glass filled with ice.

Garnish with raspberry and basil leaf.

Pro Tip A shrub is basically a vinegar and fruit syrup. I use apple cider vinegar when making shrubs, but any vinegar you like will make a great one. The process is simple: Bring 1 cup vinegar and 1 cup sugar to a simmer to dissolve, then remove from heat and add in the fruit, in this case, about 1.5 cups of raspberry (fresh or frozen). Allow to steep until cool and then purée in a blender. Pour into a sealable jar and it will keep under refrigeration for several weeks. As a general rule, I strain any shrubs that feature seeds like raspberry, blackberry or kiwi. Shrubs are useful in cocktails but are also nice as a quick refresher over ice with seltzer or sparkling wine—they make great gifts! You can make compound shrubs also, like strawberry-jalapeño or pear-cinnamon, etc. Experiment with flavors you like and see what you come up with!

SCROOGE: LET US DEAL WITH THE EVICTION NOTICES FOR TOMORROW, MR. CRATCHIT.

KERMIT: UH, TOMORROW'S CHRISTMAS, SIR.

SCROOGE: VERY WELL. YOU MAY GIFT WRAP THEM.

—The Muppet Christmas Carol

YOUTHFUL EXPRESSION

Featuring Ramazzotti,

a kola nut amaro with a Dr. Pepper-like flavor, this drink tastes like your early drinking days and comes with only half the mistakes you used to make. Unless you have more than one. Go own the Naughty List like a pro.

2 dashes Bittercube Cherry Bark Vanilla Bitters

I oz Ramazzotti

I oz bourbon

I oz London dry gin

Seltzer

* Combine first four ingredients in a collins glass.
* Add ice and gently stir to chill.
* Pour seltzer down the spiral of a bar spoon to fill.

No garnish.

TODD: WHERE DO YOU THINK YOU'RE GONNA PUT A TREE THAT BIG?

CLARK: BEND OVER AND I'LL SHOW YOU.

—National Lampoon's Christmas Vacation

HERBALIST TEA

Curl up by the fire

with this festive brew that
features Amaro dell'Erborista,
an herbal bitter with notes of
smoked tea and bitter honey.
Don't get too close, though—that
ugly sweater looks flammable.

* Add all ingredients to a warmed mug.

Garnish with clove-studded lemon wedge.

2 dashes 18.21 Lemon
Ginger Tincture

2 oz piping hot water

0.25 oz ginger syrup
(see pg. 67)

0.25 oz lemon juice

0.5 oz peated scotch
whiskey (I use
Laphroaig)

1.5 oz dell'Erborista

Pro Tip If you can't find dell'Erborista in your area you have
two options: Move, or swap it out for something else. Like
most amaros, dell'Erborista is tough to replicate exactly. I
recommend swapping in Suze as an amaro, or ditching the
hot water in favor of Lapsang souchong tea.

SHARPIE MUSTACHE

Much like a flying reindeer, gin and whiskey make for an unlikely but powerful combination. Pace yourself, though, or you risk waking up under the Christmas tree wearing a Sharpie mustache of your own.

* Stir with plenty of ice to chill and dilute.
* Serve up or in a 100ml glass flask.

Garnish with an orange twist.

2 dashes Bittermens 'Elemakule Tiki Bitters

0.75 oz Amaro Meletti

0.75 oz Bonal Gentiane Quina

0.75 oz London dry gin (Beefeater)

0.75 oz 100° rye whiskey (Rittenhouse)

Pro Tip Planning on getting someone on your gift list a flask for the holidays? Why not fill it with one of these delicious drinks? They'll remember the gesture for years to come, provided they can recall who gave it to them.

BRAWNY MAN

When you're sick of the sweets, show everyone at Christmas you're a grown-ass adult by downing this ultra-bitter brew that'll sober you up from the Christmas spirit overload and still get you buzzed.

⁕ Stir all ingredients with ice to chill and dilute.

⁕ Strain into a chilled rocks glass without ice.

Garnish with an orange twist.

0.25 oz J. Rieger Caffè Amaro

0.75 oz peated scotch

0.75 oz Punt e Mes

0.75 oz Gran Classico

0.75 oz Varnelli Amaro Dell'Erborista

5 Christmas Movie Characters You'd Want to Grab a Drink With

If they were real, these Christmas characters would be great to converse with over a cocktail or three.

Buddy the Elf, Elf

If you get a few pints in him, you might be able to convince Buddy to create several last-minute Etch-a-Sketch masterpieces for the folks on your list.

Clark Griswold, National Lampoon's Christmas Vacation

His drive to make this holiday the best ever means he's likely to pick up the tab if you compliment his light display. Plus, the guy could use a drink.

Yukon Cornelius, Rudolph the Red-Nosed Reindeer

This bearded outdoorsman bested a yeti. He can easily get you past a surly doorman.

Jack Skellington, The Nightmare Before Christmas

The jolly skeleton "Pumpkin King" is merry in a goth sort of way. Here's hoping his massive skull face scares the bartender into giving us free drinks (especially if his ghost dog comes along).

The Old Man, A Christmas Story

At the least, he has great taste in lamps.

DISCO BALL

Screw creepy mistletoe.

Hang up a disco ball instead
and get the party started with
a round of these. Dance like no
one's watching even though they
will be because you're drunk.

* Stir first five ingredients in a mixing
glass with plenty of ice to chill and
dilute.
* Strain into a chilled cocktail glass.

Lemon twist, discarded.

2 dashes Devil's Larder
Chamomile bitters

0.5 oz Green
Chartreuse

0.5 oz Yellow
Chartreuse

1 oz blanc vermouth

1 oz mezcal

THE POLAR EXPRESS

Who needs a magical train to take you to the North Pole when you can sit back, enjoy a few of these and let Santa come to you? Let the man do his job.

* Shake all ingredients with plenty of ice to chill and dilute.
* Double strain into a stemmed cocktail glass.

1.5 oz London dry gin (you won't hurt my feelings if you'd prefer vodka)

I oz crisp dry white wine

0.5 oz Curaçao

I tsp orange marmalade

Pro Tip If stores in your area are closed for the holidays, sometimes you have to improvise. Don't be afraid to tinker with fruit-based condiments in lieu of fruit juice, or to use a different (but similar) spot of booze in the place of a suggested ingredient. Pinot grigio and pinot gris aren't the same, but one will work for the other in a pinch. Whiskey and brandy aren't the same, but if you have one and not the other, who knows? You might create a substitute that works better for you than the real thing. Just don't go too far and swap in mustard for custard.

SHANDY CLAWS

Chug a few of these

on Christmas Eve and you'll be slurring by the time Santa squeezes down that chimney. Good luck getting his name right.

* Pour all ingredients into a tall pilsner glass.

Garnish with a lemon wedge dipped in cinnamon sugar.

4 oz of your favorite light-bodied crisp beer

4 oz lemon-lime soda

0.75 oz Goldschläger (or Fireball or other cinnamon liqueur)

WHITE CHRISTMAS

Snow is overrated.

You know it, I know it, everyone but Bing freaking Crosby knows it. What we're dreaming of is rum—white rum to be exact.

* Pour all ingredients into a shaker tin and shake vigorously for 10 seconds to emulsify the egg white.
* Add plenty of ice and shake vigorously for an additional 30 seconds.
* Double strain into a stemmed cocktail glass.

I small egg white

1.5 oz white rum (Banks 5)

0.5 oz Velvet Falernum

0.5 oz lime juice

0.5 oz pineapple juice

SANTA'S LITTLE HELPER

When you're staring down a stack of presents to wrap and guests are nearly knocking on your door, knock back one of these and get elfing busy courtesy of coffee and a Homer Simpson-sized shot of booze.

2 dashes Dale DeGroff's Pimento Bitters

0.5 oz strong coffee

⅛ oz Grade B maple syrup

1.5 oz bourbon (Evan Williams Single Barrel is a steal of a whiskey)

* Add all ingredients to a double rocks glass.
* Add a large cube of ice and gently stir just to incorporate the components.

Garnish with a flamed orange twist.

Pro Tip I will continue to sing the praises of Dale DeGroff's Pimento Aromatic Bitters until they are as well-known and widely available as Angostura. If there's a cocktail connoisseur on your gift list, you can end your brainstorming about what to get them right now. They'll love it.

FRANK: MANY CHRISTMASES AGO, I WENT TO BUY A DOLL FOR MY SON. I REACHED FOR THE LAST ONE THEY HAD, BUT SO DID ANOTHER MAN. AS I RAINED BLOWS UPON HIM, I REALIZED THERE HAD TO BE ANOTHER WAY.

KRAMER: WHAT HAPPENED TO THE DOLL?

FRANK: IT WAS DESTROYED. BUT OUT OF THAT, A NEW HOLIDAY WAS BORN.

A FESTIVUS FOR THE REST-OF-US.

—Seinfeld

FEATS OF STRENGTH

You've aired your
grievances, now bring your loved
ones together the way only
booze and the Festivus pole can
as you prepare to show off your
physical prowess. Just make sure
no one's recording your antics
or you'll go viral. That'd be a
Festivus miracle.

2 dashes Dale DeGroff's
Pimento Bitters

0.5 oz pineapple juice

0.75 oz lemon juice

0.5 oz cranberry juice

0.5 oz simple syrup

1.5 oz Pierre Ferrand
Cognac (or your
favorite brandy)

＊ Shake with plenty of ice to chill and
dilute.

＊ Strain into fresh ice in a double rocks
glass.

*Garnish with a grapefruit twist
and a dash of cinnamon.*

PROPS MAN: I CAN'T GET THE ANTLERS GLUED TO THIS LITTLE GUY. WE TRIED CRAZY GLUE, BUT IT DON'T WORK.

FRANK: DID YOU TRY STAPLES?

—*Scrooged*

JUGBAND JUICE

This fruity drink harkens back to a simpler time. The blackstrap rum will have you wanting to put the band back together for Christmas faster than you can say "washtub bass." Serve this in a jug and drink up to see how the notes change. Otters not included.

* Shake all ingredients with plenty of ice to chill and dilute.
* Strain onto fresh ice.

Garnish with a pineapple wedge.

1.5 oz pineapple juice

0.75 oz campari

0.5 oz simple syrup

0.5 oz fresh ruby grapefruit juice

1.5 oz blackstrap rum (Gosling's or Cruzan)

Punches
OF FUN

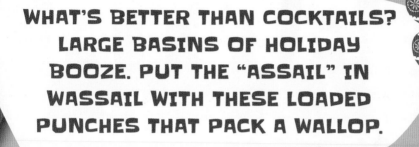

WHAT'S BETTER THAN COCKTAILS? LARGE BASINS OF HOLIDAY BOOZE. PUT THE "ASSAIL" IN WASSAIL WITH THESE LOADED PUNCHES THAT PACK A WALLOP.

"I GOTTA TELL YOU *SANTA, there's something ABOUT THIS PLACE that doesn't seem quite... KOSHER.*"

—Jingle All the Way

MELE KALIKIMAKA

A few cups of this

Hawaiian Punch for adults will
be sure to send you on your
own Christmas vacation. Just
try to steer clear of any angry
squirrels.

* For best results, chill all the liquids
overnight before beginning.
* Add all liquid ingredients to a large
punch bowl. Whip vigorously with a
whisk. (An immersion or stick blender
works great. So does a standard
blender, if you work in batches.)
Add one large block of ice as well as
plenty of service-size ice cubes into the
bowl.
* Feel free to decorate with fresh
orange and pineapple slices.

Garnish with freshly grated nutmeg.

Makes approximately 12 6-oz servings.

25 oz dark rum
(Pusser's is traditional
but your favorite will
do)

32 oz pineapple juice
(fresh is best, then
Looza, then Dole)

8 oz cream of coconut
(Do not confuse with
coconut cream; I like
Coco López)

8 oz orange juice

"LOOK, CHARLIE, let's face it. We all know that CHRISTMAS is a big commercial racket. IT'S RUN BY a big Eastern syndicate, YOU KNOW."

—A Charlie Brown Christmas

HO HO HOT TODDY

Keep the holiday blues and the Saturday sniffles at bay all season long with this herbal, time-tested pick-me-up. Add more bourbon to quiet a lingering cold or family member.

8 bags Earl Grey tea

8 oz clover honey

8 thyme sprigs

3 rosemary sprigs

24 oz water

8 oz cranberry juice

32 oz bourbon

0.5 oz orange bitters

* Before serving, combine tea, honey, herbs and water in a sauce pot and bring to a gentle simmer. After 5 minutes, remove the tea bags and discard. Allow to cool to room temperature before straining out and discarding the herbs.
* When you're ready to serve, in a larger pot, combine tea mixture with bourbon, cranberry juice and bitters. Gently heat without bringing to a simmer. Ladle into mugs and serve. (This also works nicely at a low temperature in a slow cooker.)

Makes approximately 18 4-oz mugs.

" LIFE IS LIKE THAT. SOMETIMES, AT THE HEIGHT OF OUR REVELRIES, WHEN OUR JOY IS AT ITS ZENITH, WHEN ALL IS MOST RIGHT WITH THE WORLD, THE MOST UNTHINKABLE DISASTERS DESCEND UPON US. "

–A Christmas Story

THE RED RYDER BB GUN

If the holidays make you want to shoot your eye out, put down the gun and grab one of these instead. After a few cups, you'll never know what hit you.

32 oz apple brandy

8 oz lemon juice

4 oz lime juice

4 oz sugar dissolved in 8 oz pomegranate juice

32 oz ginger beer (I like Reeds because it's spicy)

* Add the first four liquid ingredients to a large punch bowl. Whip vigorously with a whisk to incorporate all ingredients. (An immersion/stick blender works great. So does a standard blender, just work in batches.)
* Add one large block of ice as well as plenty of service-size ice cubes into the bowl. Pour in the ginger beer.

Garnish with thin slices of crisp red apple.

Makes approximately 20 5-oz servings.

“I planned out our whole DAY: First, we'll make SNOW ANGELS for two hours and then we'll go ICE SKATING and then we'll eat a WHOLE ROLL of Toll House COOKIE DOUGH as fast as we can and then to finish we'll SNUGGLE.”

—Elf

COTTON-HEADED NINNY MUGGINS

You don't need to be an elf to enjoy this drink, but you might want to make extra—Santa's little helpers are thirsty. (Bonus points if you correctly guess the three elf food groups missing from this list.)

* In a blender, process the lime juice and strawberries until smooth. Pour into a punch bowl with all other liquids except sparkling wine, and whisk to combine.
* Add one large block of ice as well as plenty of service-size ice cubes. When ready to serve, ladle into a glass over ice and top with sparkling wine.

Garnish with sliced strawberries and a puff of pink cotton candy when ready to serve.

Makes approximately 15 4-oz servings.

20 oz blanco tequila (I use Altos)

½ pint strawberries

10 oz lime juice

7.5 oz triple sec

1.5 oz agave syrup

25 oz (one 750mL bottle) sparkling rosé

[ANSWER KEY]
Candy, candy canes and candy corn. You win: More booze!

New Year's Eve Party Dos and Don'ts

Resolve to avoid any major mistakes.

DO Indulge in the free booze and finger foods.
DON'T Bring Tupperware to smuggle appetizers home in your purse.

DO Sing "Auld Lang Syne," even if you can't remember its name.
DON'T Hook up with an "auld acquaintance" if you can't remember theirs.

DO Watch the ball drop.
DON'T Drop your drink.

DO Pet the host's dog.
DON'T Steal the host's dog.

DO Buy a fancy suit or dress for the occasion.
DON'T Forget to cut off the tags.

DO Tune in to see the revelers in Times Square.
DON'T Wear a diaper in solidarity.

DO Tell others what your resolution will be.
DON'T Tell others what their resolution should be.

DO Ring in the New Year by setting off fireworks.
DON'T Ring in the New Year by setting off fire alarms.

DO Count down to midnight.
DON'T Forget to check the time.

DO Thank everyone for coming to your shindig.
DON'T Tell them to leave at 12:01.

WHAT THE DICKENS?

Watch as whiskey wipes away the ghosts of Christmases past, present and yet to come with this strong, sweet drink. Pace yourself, though. You've still got to be ready for the New Year's baby.

5 oz cranberry juice

4 oz sugar

10 oz tart cherry juice

20 oz George Dickel Tennessee whiskey

22 oz lemon-lime soda

* Dissolve the sugar in cranberry juice and pour into a punch bowl. Add all other liquids except the soda and whisk to combine.
* Add one large block of ice as well as plenty of service-size ice cubes into the bowl.
* Serve over ice and top with soda.

Garnish with fresh rosemary sprigs and fresh cranberries.

Makes approximately 12 5-oz servings.

MAYOR: HOW HORRIBLE OUR CHRISTMAS WILL BE!

JACK: NO.... HOW JOLLY.

MAYOR: OH. HOW JOLLY OUR CHRISTMAS WILL BE!

—The Nightmare Before Christmas

A VISION OF SUGAR PLUMS

No creatures will be stirring after a few rounds of this punch.

＊ Add all liquids to a punch bowl and whisk to combine. Add one large block of ice or an ice ring.

Garnish with slices of pineapple and dark-skinned plums.

Makes approximately 15 4-oz servings.

5 oz lime juice

15 oz pineapple juice

12 oz Chambord

20 oz brandy

UPPERCUT

When your head is
buzzing with Christmas carols, knock yourself out with an Uppercut. At the very least, the notes of apple and cinnamon will keep you warm and fuzzy.

* Build in a glass over ice and top with cider. Scale up the ingredients by the number of guests you expect to serve, allowing for two drinks per guest.

Garnish with sliced apples and grapes.

2 dashes Greenbar Apple Bitters

0.5 oz lemon juice

0.25 oz orange juice

0.25 oz Becherovka (or cinnamon clove syrup, page 68)

0.75 oz Applejack

I oz bourbon

Hard cider

Pro Tip I recommend using a heavy-hitting bourbon like Wild Turkey, which at 101 proof can handle considerable dilution from the juices. Applejack provides a fruity foil to the mix as well. If you can locate Becherovka, an herbal liqueur from the Czech Republic, you'll immediately fall in love with its sharp notes of cinnamon and clove. If not, cinnamon clove syrup will do the job.

GRANDMOTHER'S TEA

Granny had the right idea when she made this brew—no wonder she was so cheery. Now you too can drown yourself in some old-fashioned holiday spirit. Just watch out for reindeer.

* Stir the first five ingredients over plenty of ice to chill and dilute. Strain into a rocks glass over fresh ice. This can easily be scaled up for a pitcher based on the number of guests you're planning to serve. Plan for two drinks per guest.

Garnish with orange and lemon twists.

I dash Bittermens Orange Cream Citrate

0.5 oz Strega

0.5 oz Amaro del Capo

I oz blanc vermouth

I oz Pierre Ferrand Cognac

RECIPE INDEX

INGREDIENT INDEX

NOTES

Cocktail: _____

Pg. _____

☐ **Naughty** ☐ Nice

Other notes: _____

_____

_____

Cocktail: _____

Pg. _____

☐ **Naughty** ☐ Nice

Other notes: _____

_____

_____

Cocktail: _____

Pg. _____

☐ **Naughty** ☐ Nice

Other notes: _____

_____

_____

Cocktail: _____

Pg. _____

☐ **Naughty** ☐ Nice

Other notes: _____

_____

_____

Cocktail: _____

Pg. _____

☐ **Naughty** ☐ Nice

Other notes: _____

_____

_____

Cocktail: _____

Pg. _____

☐ **Naughty** ☐ Nice

Other notes: _____

_____

_____

Cocktail: _____

Pg. _____

☐ **Naughty** ☐ Nice

Other notes: _____

_____

_____

Cocktail: _____

Pg. _____

☐ **Naughty** ☐ Nice

Other notes: _____

_____

_____

Cocktail: _____

Pg. ____

☐ **Naughty** ☐ Nice

Other notes: _____

_____

_____

Cocktail: _____

Pg. ____

☐ **Naughty** ☐ Nice

Other notes: _____

_____

_____

Cocktail: _____

Pg. ____

☐ **Naughty** ☐ Nice

Other notes: _____

_____

_____

Cocktail: _____

Pg. ____

☐ **Naughty** ☐ Nice

Other notes: _____

_____

_____

Cocktail: _____

Pg. ____

☐ **Naughty** ☐ Nice

Other notes: _____

_____

_____

Cocktail: _____

Pg. ____

☐ **Naughty** ☐ Nice

Other notes: _____

_____

_____

Cocktail: _____

Pg. ____

☐ **Naughty** ☐ Nice

Other notes: _____

_____

_____

Cocktail: _____

Pg. ____

☐ **Naughty** ☐ Nice

Other notes: _____

_____

_____

NOTES

Cocktail: _____

Pg. ____

☐ Naughty ☐ Nice

Other notes: _____

_____

_____

Cocktail: _____

Pg. ____

☐ Naughty ☐ Nice

Other notes: _____

_____

_____

Cocktail: _____

Pg. ____

☐ Naughty ☐ Nice

Other notes: _____

_____

_____

Cocktail: _____

Pg. ____

☐ Naughty ☐ Nice

Other notes: _____

_____

_____

Cocktail: _____

Pg. ____

☐ Naughty ☐ Nice

Other notes: _____

_____

_____

Cocktail: _____

Pg. ____

☐ Naughty ☐ Nice

Other notes: _____

_____

_____

Cocktail: _____

Pg. ____

☐ Naughty ☐ Nice

Other notes: _____

_____

_____

Cocktail: _____

Pg. ____

☐ Naughty ☐ Nice

Other notes: _____

_____

_____

Cocktail: _____

Pg. _____

☐ **Naughty** ☐ Nice

Other notes: _____

_____

_____

Cocktail: _____

Pg. _____

☐ **Naughty** ☐ Nice

Other notes: _____

_____

_____

Cocktail: _____

Pg. _____

☐ **Naughty** ☐ Nice

Other notes: _____

_____

_____

Cocktail: _____

Pg. _____

☐ **Naughty** ☐ Nice

Other notes: _____

_____

_____

Cocktail: _____

Pg. _____

☐ **Naughty** ☐ Nice

Other notes: _____

_____

_____

Cocktail: _____

Pg. _____

☐ **Naughty** ☐ Nice

Other notes: _____

_____

_____

Cocktail: _____

Pg. _____

☐ **Naughty** ☐ Nice

Other notes: _____

_____

_____

Cocktail: _____

Pg. _____

☐ **Naughty** ☐ Nice

Other notes: _____

_____

_____

NOTES

Cocktail: _____

Pg. ____

☐ **Naughty** ☐ Nice

Other notes: _____

_____

_____

Cocktail: _____

Pg. ____

☐ **Naughty** ☐ Nice

Other notes: _____

_____

_____

Cocktail: _____

Pg. ____

☐ **Naughty** ☐ Nice

Other notes: _____

_____

_____

Cocktail: _____

Pg. ____

☐ **Naughty** ☐ Nice

Other notes: _____

_____

_____

Cocktail: _____

Pg. ____

☐ **Naughty** ☐ Nice

Other notes: _____

_____

_____

Cocktail: _____

Pg. ____

☐ **Naughty** ☐ Nice

Other notes: _____

_____

_____

Cocktail: _____

Pg. ____

☐ **Naughty** ☐ Nice

Other notes: _____

_____

_____

Cocktail: _____

Pg. ____

☐ **Naughty** ☐ Nice

Other notes: _____

_____

_____

Cocktail: _____

Pg. ____

☐ Naughty ☐ Nice

Other notes: _____

_____

_____

Cocktail: _____

Pg. ____

☐ Naughty ☐ Nice

Other notes: _____

_____

_____

Cocktail: _____

Pg. ____

☐ Naughty ☐ Nice

Other notes: _____

_____

_____

Cocktail: _____

Pg. ____

☐ Naughty ☐ Nice

Other notes: _____

_____

_____

Cocktail: _____

Pg. ____

☐ Naughty ☐ Nice

Other notes: _____

_____

_____

Cocktail: _____

Pg. ____

☐ Naughty ☐ Nice

Other notes: _____

_____

_____

Cocktail: _____

Pg. ____

☐ Naughty ☐ Nice

Other notes: _____

_____

_____

Cocktail: _____

Pg. ____

☐ Naughty ☐ Nice

Other notes: _____

_____

_____

"Merry Christmas to all,
and to all a good nightcap!"

Acknowledgments

First off, thanks to you for reading this book. Without you, there'd be one fewer copy sold. And what are the holidays for if not celebrating a quality purchase? Secondly, thanks to the incomparable staff at Amor y Amargo, the best gift a guy could ask for, as well as all the women and men who've tended to me over the years over their bars. Without the opportunity to sit and talk with you while watching you work, I'd never have amassed enough information to fill more than a matchbook. I wish all of you a wonderful holiday season, a Happy New Year and may every shift be good, prosperous and Grinch free. May your days (and nights) be merry and bright.

Finally, to Santa Claus. Thanks for sneaking into my house all these years. If I leave cocktails for you and kibble for the deer maybe you'll visit my house first next year?

SOTHER TEAGUE is an award-winning bartender, instructor and beverage director for Overthrow Hospitality living in New York City. He is the author of *I'm Just Here for the Drinks*, available wherever books are sold. He can often be found behind the bar at Amor y Amargo and can be heard on his weekly radio broadcast and podcast The Speakeasy on Heritage Radio Network.

Find me: @CreativeDrunk
Hear me: @SpeakeasyPodcast
Let me know:
#ShowingTheWork
#AlcoHolidays

Topix Media Lab
For inquiries, call 646-449-8614

Copyright 2022 by Sother Teague

Published by Topix Media Lab
14 Wall Street, Suite 3C
New York, NY 10005

Printed in China

ISBN-13: 978-1-956403-32-9
ISBN-10: 1-956403-32-9

CEO Tony Romando

Vice President & Publisher Phil Sexton   **Chief Content Officer** Jeff Ashworth
Senior Vice President of Sales & New Markets Tom Mifsud   **Director of Editorial Operations** Courtney Kerrigan
Vice President of Retail Sales & Logistics Linda Greenblatt   **Creative Director** Susan Dazzo
Chief Financial Officer Vandana Patel   **Photo Director** Dave Weiss
Manufacturing Director Nancy Puskuldjian   **Executive Editor** Tim Baker
Financial Analyst Matthew Quinn
Digital Marketing & Strategy Manager Elyse Gregov

Features Editor Trevor Courneen
Associate Editor Juliana Sharaf
Assistant Managing Editor Tara Sherman
Designers Glen Karpowich, Mikio Sakai
Copy Editor & Fact Checker Madeline Raynor
Junior Designer Alyssa Bredin Quirós
Assistant Photo Editor Jenna Addesso

All illustrations: Shutterstock

Indexing by R studio T, NYC

1C-H22-1